Women's Right to Vote

CORNERSTONES OF FREEDOM

SECOND SERIES

Elaine Landau

Children's Press
An Imprint of Scholastic Inc.
New York • Toronto • London • Auckland • Sydney
Mexico City • New Delhi • Hong Kong
Danbury, Connecticut

Photographs © 2005: Art Resource, NY/Edmund Charles
Tarbell/National Portrait Gallery, Smithsonian Institution: 33; Corbis
Images: cover, 5, 6, 8, 17, 22, 27, 34, 35, 38, 41, 44 bottom center,
45 (Bettmann), 7, 37 (Hulton-Deutsch Collection), 14 (Napo Sarony/
Bettmann), 3, 12, 26, 28, 44 left; Culver Pictures/Sy Seidman Collec-
tion: 13; Getty Images/Topical Press Agency/Hulton Archive: 36, 40;
Library of Congress: 11 bottom (R. W. Johnston Studios), 9, 11 top, 15,
16, 20, 23, 24, 25, 30, 31, 32, 44 right; North Wind Picture Archives:
29; Sophia Smith Collection, Smith College, Northampton, MA: 4;
Stock Montage, Inc.: 10, 19.

Library of Congress Cataloging-in-Publication Data
Landau, Elaine.
  Women's right to vote / Elaine Landau.
    p. cm. — (Cornerstones of freedom. Second series)
  Includes bibliographical references and index.
  ISBN-13: 978-0-516-23639-1 (lib. bdg.)   978-0-531-18833-0 (pbk.)
  ISBN-10: 0-516-23639-3 (lib. bdg.)   0-531-18833-7 (pbk.)
  1. Suffragists—United States—Biography—Juvenile literature.
2. Women—Suffrage—United States—History—Juvenile literature.
I. Title. II. Series.
  JK1898.5.L35 2005
  324.6'23'0973—dc22   2004017705

SCHOLASTIC, CHILDREN'S PRESS, CORNERSTONES OF FREEDOM™, and
associated logos are trademarks and/or registered trademarks of Scholastic Inc.

16 17 18 R 21 20 19 18 17   62

Scholastic Inc., 557 Broadway, New York, NY 10012.

J ULY 19, 1848, SEEMED LIKE THE hottest day of the year. But the weather didn't stop the many horse-drawn carriages from pulling up to Wesleyan Chapel in Seneca Falls, New York. About three hundred people arrived in town that day. They were there to attend the first public conference on women's rights ever held in the United States.

★　★　★　★

THE FIRST CONVENTION

EVER CALLED TO DISCUSS THE

Civil and Political Rights of Women,

SENECA FALLS, N. Y., JULY 19, 20, 1848.

———

WOMAN'S RIGHTS CONVENTION.

———

A Convention to discuss the social, civil, and religious condition and rights of woman will be held in the Wesleyan Chapel, at Seneca Falls, N. Y., on Wednesday and Thursday, the 19th and 20th of July current; commencing at 10 o'clock A. M. During the first day the meeting will be exclusively for women, who are earnestly invited to attend. The public generally are invited to be present on the second day, when Lucretia Mott, of Philadelphia, and other ladies and gentlemen, will address the Convention.*

* This call was published in the *Seneca County Courier*, July 14, 1848, without any signatures. The movers of this Convention, who drafted the call, the declaration and resolutions were Elizabeth Cady Stanton, Lucretia Mott, Martha C. Wright, Mary Ann McClintock, and Jane C. Hunt.

This summons was published in the Seneca County Courier on July 14, 1848. It announced the first women's rights convention at Seneca Falls, New York.

* * * *

Both men and women came. All had answered an open invitation appearing in the *Seneca County Courier*. It announced a conference to discuss "the social, civil, and religious . . . rights of women."

Elizabeth Cady Stanton, a young married woman, had placed the invitation in the paper. Known for her rebellious spirit, she was one of the women behind the Seneca Falls conference. Another important woman involved in its planning was Lucretia Mott. Stanton had met Mott in 1840. At the time, both women were **abolitionists,** working hard to end slavery.

Yet they knew that more needed to be done. Someone had to speak up for women's rights. They, along with a number of other women, decided to take on the challenge.

Stanton made sure that the women were well-prepared for their first conference. She drew up a special document called the Declaration of Sentiments and Resolutions. Based on the Declaration of Independence, Stanton's document began with the idea that all men and women are created equal.

Elizabeth Cady Stanton, shown here speaking at Seneca Falls, was one of the leaders of the women's rights movement.

5

★ ★ ★ ★

A NEED FOR CHANGE

The Seneca Falls conference was an important event for the nation's women. For years, they had been treated as second-class citizens. While women often worked as hard as men, they enjoyed few rights. The meeting at Seneca Falls marked the birth of a much larger movement—a movement that would one day affect how women would be seen and treated both at home and in the workplace.

In preparing her Declaration of Sentiments and Resolutions, Stanton listed eighteen **injustices** endured by women. These called attention to the unfairness of a system

Women test new phonograph rolls before they are shipped to stores.

in which males largely controlled females. In those days, once a woman married, everything she had belonged to her husband. If she worked, her salary went to him. If there was a divorce, the children stayed with their father. Even a woman's clothing was considered her husband's property.

Stanton also had a list of resolutions, or ideas for change. She wanted these to be discussed and approved by those attending the Seneca Falls Conference. Stanton hoped to develop a strong group of people who were united on some common goals. She felt that this could be the start of a vital movement. On July 20, the second day of the convention, it looked as if that would happen. One by one, each resolution was discussed and adopted—until they reached the ninth.

Voting rights would prove to be one of the most important aspects of the women's movement.

THE NINTH RESOLUTION

Resolved: that it is the duty of the women of this country to secure to themselves their sacred right to elective franchise.

Simply put, the ninth resolution asked that women be given the right to vote. After the resolution was read, an uproar began almost instantly. Many people claimed that

7

Many people feared that asking for the right to vote would incite further ridicule from outsiders. This illustration shows Lucretia Mott being surrounded by an angry mob of men.

this demand went too far. It was too **radical,** they said. Others felt that it would surely make the conference look foolish. They feared that the people attending it would not be taken seriously.

Elizabeth Cady Stanton wasn't shaken by their reaction. In fact, she had expected it. Even Stanton's husband, an attorney who had long been an abolitionist, had been shocked by the ninth resolution. He'd strongly urged his wife to remove it from the document. When she refused, he threatened to leave town before the conference and not return until it was over.

Stanton had gotten a similar response from Lucretia Mott. Mott felt that her friend wanted too much too soon. She'd told Stanton, "Oh Lizzie, if thou demands that, thou will make us ridiculous. We must go slowly." But Elizabeth Cady Stanton refused to budge.

* * * *

The ninth resolution caused a long and heated debate at the conference. Stanton stressed that the right to vote would make women truly equal decision makers in their own nation. Even Frederick Douglass agreed. Douglass was a runaway slave who had become well-known and respected in the antislavery movement. He had come to the Seneca Falls Conference to support women in their struggle for equality. Douglass believed that Stanton was right and was not afraid to say so.

To Stanton's relief, the ninth resolution passed when it was voted on. It only passed by a few votes, but that didn't matter. It was still an important step forward.

Nevertheless, the women had a long way to go. The fight for women's rights remained a tiny and unpopular movement until the end of the nineteenth century. Even then, there were only 13,000 females in the women's movement as compared with 100,000 women active in the **temperance movement.** Yet those leading the struggle refused to give up. They were determined to turn things around.

Frederick Douglass, a respected abolitionist, provided a strong voice in support of the women's rights movement.

Abigail Adams was among the first women in the United States to openly question the role of women in society.

EARLY WARNINGS

Women had longed for equality for years. In the late 1700s, Abigail Adams advised her husband, future president John Adams, as he helped to shape our nation's laws. She told him to "remember the ladies and be more generous to them than your ancestors." She added, "If particular attention is not paid to the ladies, we are determined to foment [start] a rebellion, and will not hold ourselves bound by any laws in which we have no representation."

THE MOVEMENT BEGINS

The women's right-to-vote movement was on its way. The females behind it, called **suffragists,** were determined to win. At the Seneca Falls Conference, Elizabeth Cady Stanton laid out the next step in her plan. "We hope this conference will be followed by a series of conferences embracing every part of this country," she said to the crowd.

* * * *

To Stanton's delight, the first National Women's Rights Conference was held in Worcester, Massachusetts, in 1850. The driving force behind this conference was a woman named Lucy Stone. Stone had graduated from Oberlin College in 1843. Having experienced the injustices endured by women, she, like Stanton, felt that something needed to be done. So she became active in the fight for women's rights.

The first national conference was a great success. More than one thousand people attended. After that, conferences were held almost every year through the 1850s. It wasn't long before increasing numbers of women were drawn to this growing movement.

Lucy Stone was a pioneer in the women's movement. She felt so strongly about it that, after marrying Henry Blackwell in 1855, she did not take her husband's name.

Oberlin College in Oberlin, Ohio, was the first college in the United States to offer admission to women.

11

"THE BLOOMER"

In the 1800s women commonly wore tight-fitting **corsets** and tightly laced dresses. But in 1851 a woman named Amelia Bloomer designed a more comfortable outfit for women. It was made up of a loose top and a short skirt worn over baggy pants that narrowed at the ankle. Known as the bloomer, the outfit was worn by some suffragists as an expression of freedom.

This illustration shows the bloomer as it looked in 1851.

IMPORTANT LEADERS

Before long, some key women became leaders of the movement. Besides Elizabeth Cady Stanton, Lucretia Mott, and Lucy Stone, another important player emerged. Her name was Susan B. Anthony.

Anthony, who chose never to marry, worked tirelessly for women's rights. She was brought up a Quaker and experienced more freedom than many young women. But it wasn't long before she saw the inequality between men and women. As a teacher, she was paid only one fifth of what male teachers were paid. When Anthony complained about it, she lost her job.

In the early 1850s, Anthony met women who were active in the women's rights movement. She formed a deep and lasting friendship with Elizabeth Cady Stanton. Stanton described Anthony as having "a broad and generous nature, and a depth of tenderness that few women possess." Together, Stanton and Anthony were determined to improve the lives of American women. In the years that followed, they lectured on the importance of the ballot and helped to start state and local women's groups.

Susan B. Anthony was born into a Quaker family and was well-educated. She was not used to having her opinions ignored.

13

This photograph of Elizabeth Cady Stanton (left) and Susan B. Anthony was taken thirty years after they met.

During the Civil War (1861–1865), their work took a backseat to the crisis at hand. Instead, much of the women's energy went toward supporting the effort to free the slaves. In 1863, Anthony and Stanton led women in collecting hundreds of thousands of signatures for a **petition.** The petition asked for a constitutional **amendment** to end slavery. In December 1865, their hard work paid off. The Thirteenth Amendment to the Constitution was adopted, abolishing slavery in the United States.

After the war, there was talk of giving former slaves the right to vote. Women's rights groups supported this idea. However, they wanted the same for women. In 1866, Stanton and Anthony formed the American Equal Rights Association. Its goal was to win the vote for both former slaves and women.

Yet before long, many of the organization's members began to feel that they'd made a mistake. They thought that insisting on voting rights for

THE PERFECT PAIR

The bond between Elizabeth Cady Stanton and Susan B. Anthony lasted more than fifty years. Stanton described their relationship in her **autobiography,** *Eighty Years and More:*

In thought and sympathy we are one, and in the division of labor we exactly complemented each other. I am the better writer, she the better critic . . . together we have made arguments that have stood unshaken through the storms of long years; arguments that no one has answered.

Emancipation Ordinance of Missouri

women would hurt their chances of winning this right for former slaves. As a result, most of the organization's work supported African American males.

This document ordered the release of all slaves in the state of Missouri in 1865. Three weeks later, the Thirteenth Amendment was proposed by Congress.

Proud members of the National Woman Suffrage Association

THE WOMEN'S MOVEMENT SPLITS

This difference in view caused a split in the women's movement. In 1869, Stanton and Anthony started a new group called the National Woman Suffrage Association (NWSA). This group was against the proposed Fifteenth Amendment, which would grant voting rights to African American males but made no mention of women.

NWSA wanted another amendment passed instead. This amendment would ensure universal suffrage, or the right to vote for everyone. The association's other goals included creating fairer divorce laws and organizing female workers into unions in order to get higher salaries. The suffragists were well-aware of the connection between money and freedom. As Stanton put it, "Woman will always be dependent until she holds a purse of her own."

The Fifteenth Amendment guaranteed all citizens—except women—the right to vote, regardless of race.

★ ★ ★ ★

REVOLUTION

In 1868, Anthony, Stanton, and other suffragists started a newspaper. This newspaper was called the *Revolution*. Stanton explained the paper's name in this way:

There would not be a better name than Revolution.

The establishing of woman on her rightful throne is the greatest revolution the world has ever known or ever will know. To bring it about is no child's play.

Lucy Stone disagreed with Stanton and Anthony's goals. That same year Lucy Stone started a less radical group called the American Woman Suffrage Association (AWSA). Stone's organization would "not attack the [proposed] Fifteenth Amendment or complicate the question of woman suffrage with side issues."

Meanwhile, in 1870 the Fifteenth Amendment to the U.S. Constitution was adopted. Stanton, Anthony, and their followers were disappointed, but the women refused to give up. The road ahead wasn't easy. At nearly every turn, they had to fight deeply held **prejudices** against women.

Many people were opposed to women's suffrage. They argued that the country would fall apart if women won the right to vote. They claimed that women were less intelligent than men and would not be able to make sound decisions at the ballot box. They even said that voting rights for women would destroy the American family. Women who were interested in politics would surely neglect their children and households.

Progress came slowly, but the women did enjoy some victories along the way. In 1869, the U.S. territory of Wyoming granted women the right to vote. In 1871, Stanton and Anthony traveled to Wyoming to visit this "land of freedom." Yet they knew that Wyoming's action was just a small step in the right direction. They were determined to see women voting across the nation.

In 1870, women in Wyoming waited in line to vote for the first time.

A BOLD STATEMENT

Soon, Anthony and Stanton decided a bold statement was needed. Anthony and fifteen other women in Rochester, New York, openly challenged the law. They voted in the November 1872 presidential election. Anthony stressed that women should be allowed to vote as a result of the Fourteenth Amendment. Adopted in 1868, this amendment

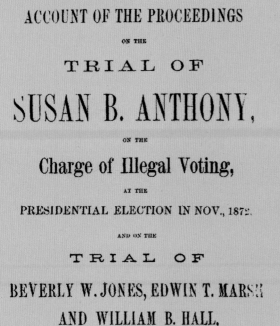

This is an excerpt from the official document charging Susan B. Anthony with the "crime" of voting in a presidential election.

ensured that all legal rights must be extended equally to all citizens. Anthony argued that women were citizens, so they had the right to vote.

Not everyone agreed. All the women, as well as the men who had allowed them to vote, were arrested within weeks. Susan B. Anthony, however, was the only one put on trial for the crime.

Anthony did not wait until her trial to tell her side of the story. To defend her position, Anthony traveled to all twenty-nine post office districts within Monroe County (New York). She stopped at each to give the following speech:

Friends and Fellow citizens: I stand before you tonight under indictment for the alleged crime of having voted at the last presidential election, without having a lawful right to vote. It shall be my work this evening to prove to you that in thus voting, I not only committed no crime, but, instead, simply exercised my citizen's rights, guaranteed to me and all United States citizens by the National Constitution. . . .

The preamble to the Federal Constitution says: "We, the people of the United States" . . . not we, the white male citizens; nor yet we, the male citizens; but we, the whole

* * * *

people who formed the Union. And it is a downright mockery to talk to women of their enjoyment of the blessings of liberty while they are denied the use of the only means of securing them provided by this democratic-republican government—the ballot.

Anthony's trial began on June 17, 1873. Her lawyer had to testify for her in court. After explaining Anthony's position, he added, "If the same act had been done by her brother under the same circumstances, the act would have been not only innocent, but honorable and laudable; but having been done by a woman it is said to be a crime. The crime, therefore, consists not in the act done, but in the simple fact that the person doing it was a woman and not a man." In the end, Anthony was found guilty and fined one hundred dollars. She refused to pay the fine.

THE WORK CONTINUES

Anthony's public protest made people even more aware of the suffrage movement. Women in different parts of the country followed her example. Others attempted to vote as a form of protest. Anthony and Stanton organized more conventions in the nation's capital. They wanted to influence as many of the country's lawmakers as possible.

Over time, suffragist leaders felt that it was important to join forces. So, in 1890, the National Woman Suffrage Association (NWSA) and the American Woman Suffrage Association (AWSA) merged. Together, they formed the National American Woman Suffrage Association (NAWSA).

Women publicly demonstrate their disapproval of the laws that did not permit them equal rights at a National Women's Suffrage Association convention.

ANNA HOWARD SHAW (1847–1919)

The suffragist leaders inspired women such as Anna Howard Shaw. In 1880, Shaw became the first female Methodist minister in the United States. She later served as president of NAWSA. Shaw explained why the fight for suffrage meant so much to her:

> To be bound by outworn customs and traditions, and be hampered by every known obstacle which could be put in one's path . . . was growing too absurd. . . . The soul within me refused to beat out its life against barred doors, and I rebelled.

In part, the merge would ensure a future for the cause. By then, women's movement leaders had actively worked for more than fifty years. These women were now older and less able to do as much as they had in their youth. They wanted to be certain that the work continued. By combining the groups, the aging leaders hoped to create a clear path for a new **generation** of suffragists to take over.

22

This poster was created for the 28th convention of the National American Woman Suffrage Association.

It was a wise move. In 1893, Lucy Stone died. Her death was followed by Elizabeth Cady Stanton's in 1902. Then in 1906, Susan B. Anthony, often called the general of the women's movement, passed away. At her last public appearance before her death, Anthony urged women not to give up the fight. She told the crowd that "failure is impossible."

★　★　★　★

As Stone, Stanton, and Anthony had hoped, their dream did not die with them. A new generation of women took over the reins. It was a group that would lead American women to victory.

THE SECOND PHASE OF THE WOMEN'S MOVEMENT

By the early 1900s, suffragists began to take a new direction. They claimed that women must be allowed to vote because females were morally superior to males. These women argued that their votes were needed to keep the country wholesome and pure.

To some degree this idea worked. By 1914, a number of states had granted women the right to vote. These included Wyoming, Colorado, Utah, Idaho, Washington, California, Arizona, Kansas, Oregon, Illinois, Nevada, and Montana. But progress was slower in other parts of the country. It became clear that an amendment to the U.S. Constitution was needed if all American women were to cast their ballots in national elections.

Susan B. Anthony and others like her inspired a new generation of suffragists.

* * * *

A TACTFUL APPROACH

One of the new figures in the women's movement was Carrie Chapman Catt. Catt was an outstanding speaker and organizer. In 1900, she followed Susan B. Anthony as the president of NAWSA. Though she had to leave the group for a short time to care for her dying husband, she returned to take an even more active role following his death. Catt knew that the struggle for women's suffrage was taking place in other countries as well. In 1902, she established the International Woman's Suffrage Association.

AN INTERNATIONAL CAUSE

Women in other countries also waged a battle for women's rights.
New Zealand women won the right to vote in 1893, while victory for
Australian women came in 1902. Sweden gave women full voting
rights in 1921. In England, women were granted partial suffrage in
1918. (Only women over age thirty could vote.) In 1928, all adult
women gained voting rights in England.

★ ★ ★ ★

Catt worked hard to draw all American women into the battle for the ballot. She actively reached out to wage-earning women. Many of these women labored more than twelve hours a day in large, crowded factories. Often they were poorly paid and worked in unsafe environments. Large numbers of

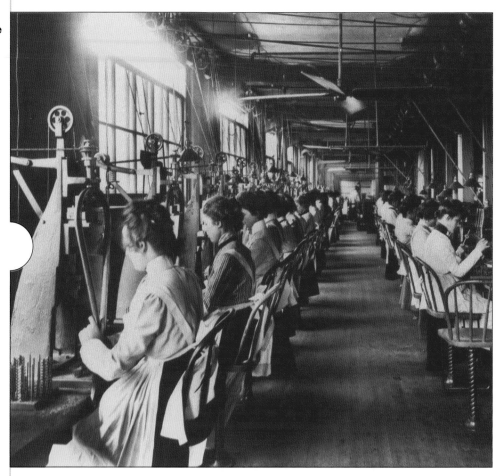

Many women were drawn to the women's rights cause in hopes of gaining better working conditions. Here, women sit at work stations at the National Cash Register Company in the early 1900s.

these women became suffragists, hoping to change things. They wanted to be able to vote for officials who would outlaw unfair and dangerous work practices. Harriot Stanton Blatch, Elizabeth Cady Stanton's daughter, succeeded in drawing many working-class women to the cause.

Catt brought increasing numbers of middle-class women into the movement as well. Among these were college-educated women who were teachers, librarians, social workers, and lawyers. These women were also anxious for change because they felt held back in their professions. They were rarely paid as much as men for their work. It was also harder for them to advance. After becoming suffragists, they often served as speakers, writers, and organizers.

Carrie Chapman Catt, center, poses with suffragists at a convention in 1914.

Catt also reached out to the wives and daughters of wealthy American industrialists, or businessmen. These women knew that they were largely powerless without their husband's or father's money. Whenever possible, they gave as much money as they could to the suffrage cause.

Catt firmly believed that **compromise** is necessary to achieve goals. She wanted her message to appeal to a broad range of people. After hearing her speak in New York State in 1914, one reporter described her speech as "factual" and

★ ★ ★ ★

delivered "so as not to offend." Carrie Chapman Catt wanted all Americans to see her cause as one that could benefit them.

CHANGE AT ANY COST

Carrie Chapman Catt's approach was nothing like Alice Paul's. Paul was another important leader in the new wave of suffragists. Born in 1885, she came from a Quaker family in New Jersey. She had earned degrees from both Swarthmore and the University of Pennsylvania. Paul had also spent time in England, where she became involved with the British women's fight for suffrage. In England it was a far more radical movement than in the United States. There the women formed picket lines, marched in parades, and even went to jail for their actions.

Alice Paul felt that American women needed to become more radical to achieve their goals. When she returned to the United States from England, she and her friend Lucy

Alice Paul was not afraid to fight for her vision of equality.

Burns joined NAWSA. She then set up a special unit of the organization in Washington, D.C. It was known as the Congressional Union. Its purpose was to convince lawmakers that women needed the vote.

Official Program WOMAN SUFFRAGE Procession

VOTES FOR WOMEN

Washington D.C. March 3, 1913

Alice Paul organized a parade in Washington, D.C., at the time of President-elect Woodrow Wilson's inauguration, hoping to get the public's attention.

A MARCH TO REMEMBER

Alice Paul was prepared to do whatever was necessary to make NAWSA's aims known in Washington, D.C. President-elect Woodrow Wilson was to be **inaugurated** in March 1913, so Paul decided to plan her own events around that time. On March 3, 1913, the day before Wilson was to take office, Paul organized a massive parade of 8,000 suffragists. They marched up Pennsylvania Avenue to the White

House. Women from every state in the Union came to the nation's capital to march.

Their march to the White House was a magnificent sight. A young woman on horseback, dressed in flowing white robes, led the procession. Behind her were divisions of women carrying colorful banners. There were marching bands and beautiful suffrage floats as well.

The parade went smoothly for the first several blocks, but trouble would soon erupt.

★ ★ ★ ★

WOMAN'S JOURNAL
AND SUFFRAGE NEWS

VOL. XLIV. NO. 10   SATURDAY, MARCH 8, 1913   FIVE CENTS

PARADE STRUGGLES TO VICTORY DESPITE DISGRACEFUL SCENES

Nation Aroused by Open Insults to Women—Cause Wins Popular Sympathy—Congress Orders Investigation—Striking Object Lesson

Washington has been disgraced. Equal suffrage has scored a great victory. Thousands of indifferent women have been aroused. Influential men are incensed and the United States Senate demands an investigation of the treatment given the suffragists at the National Capital on Monday.

Ten thousand women from all over the country had planned a magnificent parade and pageant to take place in Washington on March 3. Artists, pageant leaders, designers, women of influence and renown were ready to give a wonderful and beautiful piece of suffrage work to the public that would throng the National Capital for the inauguration festivities. The suffragists were ready; the whole procession started down Pennsylvania avenue, when the police protection, that had been promised, failed them, and a disgraceful scene followed. The crowd surged into the space which had been marked off for the paraders, and the leaders of the suffrage movement were compelled to push their way through a mob of the worst elements in Washington and vicinity.

Women were spit upon, slapped in the face, tripped up, pelted with burning cigar stubs, and insulted by jeers and obscene language too vile to print or repeat.

The cause of all the trouble is apparent when the facts are known. The police authorities in Washington opposed every attempt to have a suffrage parade at all. Having been forbidden a place in the inaugural procession, the suffragists asked to have a procession of their own on March 3. They were finally told that they could have a procession but that it could not be on Pennsylvania avenue, but must be on a side street. At last they got permission to have the suffrage parade on the avenue, and asked that traffic be excluded from the street during the parade. For a long time this was denied, and only on Saturday were they successful.

Everything was at last arranged; it was a glorious day; ten thousand women were ready to do their part to make the parade beautiful to behold, to make it a credit to womanhood and to demonstrate the strength of the movement for their enfranchisement.

The police were determined, however, and they had their way. Their attempt to afford the marchers protection and keep the space of the avenue free for the suffrage procession was the flimsiest sham. Police officers stood by with folded arms and grinned while the picked women of the land were insulted and roughly abused by an ignorant and uncouth mob.

Miss Alice Paul and other suffragists were compelled to drive their automobiles down the avenue to separate the crowds so the suffragists with the banners and floats could pass. The police officials say their force was inadequate to handle the crowds, but it is noted that there was no disorder on the avenue during the inaugural procession. It is stated that federal troops were offered to the chief of police for the suffrage procession, but that he refused their aid.

At any rate, assistance was finally

AMENDMENT WINS IN NEW JERSEY

Easy Victory in Assembly 46 to 5—Equal Suffrage Enthusiasm Runs High

The New Jersey Legislature passed the woman suffrage amendment in the Assembly last week by a vote of 46 to 5. The Senate had already voted favorably 14 to 5.

A large delegation of suffragists crowded the galleries, and when the overwhelming vote was announced there was a scene of great enthusiasm. Women stood in their seats and waved handkerchiefs and "votes for women" flags and cheered themselves hoarse.

Dr. Jekyll Becomes Mr. Hyde

Opposition was confined exclusively to the old sentimental arguments.

(Continued on Page 79)

MICHIGAN AGAIN CAMPAIGN STATE

Senate Passes Suffrage Amendment 26 to 5 and Battle Is Now On

Michigan is again a campaign State after a short lapse of four months. The amendment will go to the voters on April 7. The State-wide feeling that the women were defrauded of victory last fall will help the suffragists.

The final action of the Legislature was taken last week, when the Senate, by a vote of 26 to 5, passed the suffrage amendment, with a slight amendment to make the requirements for foreign-born women the same as those for male immigrants.

Governor Watches Debate

The debate in the Senate lasted an hour and a quarter, and was characterized by the persistent efforts of Senator Weadock and a few others to tack on crippling amendments. Several suggestions, including the disabling of women for holding office or serving on juries, were voted down in quick succession.

Gov. Ferris was among the visitors who crowded the chamber and gallery. Mrs. Clara B. Arthur, Mrs. Thomas R. Henderson and Mrs. Wilbur Brotherton, of Detroit; Mrs. Jennie Law Hardy, of Tecumseh, and other State leaders were present, supported by a large delegation of Lansing suffragists.

The final stand of the opposition was made by Senator Murfin in the hope of putting off the submission till November, 1914, and this also failed.

Of the five who opposed the measure on the final roll-call, three were from Detroit.

A complete campaign of organization and education has been mapped out by the State Association. The

(Continued on Page 74.)

The front page of the *Woman's Journal and Suffrage News* featured a story about the parade, stating that "the cause wins popular sympathy."

However, what began as a peaceful event didn't stay that way. The crowd became unruly. Some of the men screamed insults at the women. Other men physically attacked the marchers, hitting them and pushing them to the ground. Even though the women had a legal permit to march, the police stood by and refused to help them.

Despite the crowd's reaction, Alice Paul was not about to give up. She was anxious to get President Wilson's support, but she didn't get very far. When pressed, Wilson had only replied, "This subject will receive my most careful consideration."

That was hardly enough for Paul. She believed that women should "hold the [political] party in power responsible" for their situation. Paul was determined to **confront** President Wilson at every turn.

Alice Paul's **combative** tactics did not sit well with Carrie Chapman Catt. In 1916, this led to another split in the women's movement. Alice Paul and her followers left the National American Woman Suffrage Association. They

THE MARCH ON MARCH 3, 1913

A Baltimore, Maryland, newspaper described the women's march on Washington, D.C., as follows:

Eight thousand women, marching in the woman suffrage pageant today, practically fought their way foot by foot up Pennsylvania Avenue, through a surging throng that completely defied Washington police, swamped the marchers, and broke their procession into little companies. . . . No [presidential] inauguration had ever produced such scenes, which in many instances amounted to nothing less than riots.

According to Alice Paul, President Woodrow Wilson was responsible for creating equal rights for women.

Leaders of the National Woman's Party gathered in Port Washington, New York.

started a more radical organization called the National Woman's Party (NWP).

THE PROTESTS CONTINUE

By the start of 1917, President Wilson had still not backed a constitutional amendment granting women the right to vote. So Alice Paul and Lucy Burns planned a series of

★　★　★　★

protests to change his mind. Paul and Burns had always worked well together. The pair was often compared to Elizabeth Cady Stanton and Susan B. Anthony. Like those earlier suffragists, Paul and Burns admired one another's dedication and bravery. Alice Paul once described Lucy Burns as being "a thousand times more **valiant** than I." Burns felt the same way about her friend.

In early 1917, members of the NWP began **picketing** the White House. For months, the women stood on the sidewalk in front of 1600 Pennsylvania Avenue. They carried banners that read: MR. PRESIDENT—WHAT WILL YOU DO FOR WOMAN SUFFRAGE and HOW LONG MUST WOMEN WAIT FOR LIBERTY? The picketers were sometimes tormented by angry passersby, who spit at them and ripped their banners.

In 1917, suffragists began picketing at the White House. This woman holds a banner addressed to President Woodrow Wilson.

By 1917, the United States had entered World War I. Some people called the women traitors for picketing the White House during wartime. But the women were not moved by that charge. They claimed that it was wrong for President Wilson to have soldiers fighting abroad "to make

35

Suffragists are arrested during protests outside the White House in 1917.

the world safe for democracy" when there was no democracy for American women at home.

In July 1917, police began arresting the White House picketers. The women had always been careful not to break any laws, so the police took them in on the charge of "obstructing [blocking] sidewalk traffic." The arrested picketers were tried, found guilty, and sent to jail.

Alice Paul described the frightful conditions she found after arriving at the lockup:

* ✷ ✷ ✷

There we found the suffragists who had preceded us, locked in cells with no fresh air. Every window was closed tight. The air in which we would be obligated to sleep was foul. There were about eighty prisoners crowded together, tier upon tier. I went to a window and tried to open it. Instantly, a group of men, prison guards, appeared; picked me up bodily, threw me into a cell and locked the door.

Later, the jailed women began a hunger strike. They hoped to call attention to their plight by refusing to eat. They argued that they were political prisoners—locked up not for breaking laws but for demanding freedom at the ballot box.

Suffragists insist that Alice Paul and others are political prisoners.

LUCY BURNS'S ORDEAL

Lucy Burns let the public know what was happening by writing down her experiences on tiny scraps of paper that she had smuggled out of jail. She described being force-fed this way:

I was held down by five people at legs, arms, and head. I refused to open my mouth. Gannon [the prison doctor] pushed [a] tube up my left nostril. . . . It [the tube] hurts nose and throat very much and makes nose bleed freely. . . . Food dumped directly into stomach feels like a ball of lead. Left nostril, throat, and muscles of neck very sore all night.

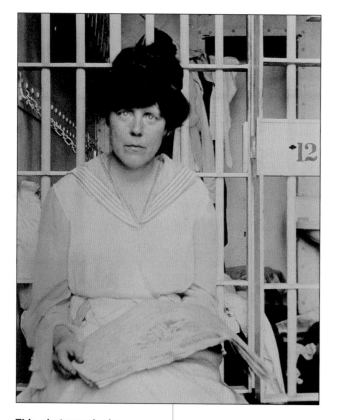

This photograph shows Lucy Burns in jail in 1917. After five weeks, she was set free.

Prison officials were determined to stop the women from using this tactic. They held the women down and force-fed them through tubes pushed up their noses and down their throats. As word of such harsh treatment spread, people's opinions began to sway in the women's favor. Eventually, President Wilson became so embarrassed by the public outcry that the women were released.

Carrie Chapman Catt felt bad for the jailed women. But she still disapproved of the NWP's methods. She and her followers in NAWSA waged the fight for the vote in a quieter way. They visited congressmen. They gave talks and wrote articles on the importance of women's suffrage. When the United States became involved in World War I, they volunteered to help with the war effort. They wanted to show that they were patriotic Americans and should not be denied the ballot.

By the close of 1917, the women's suffrage movement had picked up a good deal of public support. Catt made a

* * * *

personal appeal to President Wilson on behalf of the women of America. He finally agreed to support a women's suffrage amendment to the Constitution. But the battle still wasn't over.

The Nineteenth Amendment granting women the right to vote did not get through Congress immediately. In a 1918 vote, it passed in the House of Representatives. The Senate was not as enthusiastic, however, and it was rejected by two votes. Things went more smoothly the following year. This time, both houses passed the amendment.

Yet the amendment still wasn't law. Next, it had to be approved by thirty-six states. The many state-level women's groups sprang into action. Carrie Chapman Catt had been working with the women in these groups to make sure they were ready to take on this challenge. Now the women visited their governors to ask for support. They answered opponents' arguments at every turn. Tennessee was the thirty-sixth state to approve the amendment. It passed there by just two votes.

At last, on August 26, 1920, the Nineteenth Amendment became part of the United States Constitution. It reads:

The right of citizens of the United States to vote shall not be denied or abridged by the United States or by any State on account of sex.

This was now the law of the land. The struggle that had gone on for seventy-two years was finally won. At last the hopes and dreams of so many women had been realized.

This is a copy of the original document approving the Nineteenth Amendment to the U.S. Constitution.

The work of these and many other courageous women paved the way for women of future generations.

The words Elizabeth Cady Stanton had spoken nearly three quarters of a century earlier had come true. American women now lived in a country where, at the ballot box, "all men and women are created equal."

Glossary

abolitionist—a person who wants to outlaw or end slavery

amendment—a change made to a document such as the U.S. Constitution

autobiography—a person's life story written by that individual

combative—eager to fight or argue

compromise—to accept something that includes part of what you hoped for and part of what others hoped for

confront—to face someone in an accusing manner

corset—a tight-fitting undergarment

generation—a time span of about thirty years

inaugurated—officially put into place, usually with a ceremony

injustice—unfairness

petition—a request signed by many people asking for a policy change

picketing—protesting by standing or parading at a certain location

prejudice—an unfair opinion about someone or something

radical—in favor of extreme political change

revolution—an uprising to dramatically change a policy or system of government

suffragist—a person who favored voting rights for women

temperance movement—a movement to stop the sale and use of alcoholic beverages

valiant—showing heroism or bravery

Timeline: Women's

1848

The first women's rights conference is held in Seneca Falls, New York.

1850

The first national women's rights convention is held in Worcester, Massachusetts.

1865

The Thirteenth Amendment to the U.S. Constitution is adopted.

1866

The American Equal Rights Association is formed.

1869

The Fourteenth Amendment to the U.S. Constitution is adopted.

1870

Elizabeth Cady Stanton and Susan B. Anthony start the National Woman Suffrage Association (NWSA); Lucy Stone begins the American Woman Suffrage Association (AWSA); Wyoming Territory grants women full and equal suffrage.

1917

On March 3, a massive women's march is held in Washington, D.C.

Suffragists are jailed for picketing the White House.

1920

The Nineteenth Amendment to the U.S. Constitution is adopted, granting women the right to vote.

Right to Vote

1872	1890	1893		1902	1906	1913
The Fifteenth Amendment to the U.S. Constitution is adopted.	Susan B. Anthony, along with fifteen other women, votes in the presidential election; she is later put on trial and found guilty of breaking the law.	The National Woman Suffrage Association and the American Woman Suffrage	Association merge to form the National American Woman Suffrage Association (NAWSA).	Lucy Stone dies.	Elizabeth Cady Stanton dies; Carrie Chapman Catt starts the International Woman's Suffrage Association.	Susan B. Anthony dies.

To Find Out More

BOOKS

Brill, Marlene Targ. *Let Women Vote!* Brookfield, CT: Millbrook Press, 1996.

Fritz, Jean. *You Want Women to Vote, Lizzie Stanton?* New York: Putnam, 1995.

Isaacs, Sally Senzell. *America in the Time of Susan B. Anthony.* Chicago: Heinemann Library, 2000.

Sullivan, George. *The Day Women Got the Vote: A Photo History of the Women's Rights Movement.* New York: Scholastic, 1994.

Weidt, Maryann N. and Amanda Sartor. *Fighting for Equal Rights: A Story about Susan B. Anthony.* Minneapolis, MN: Lerner Publishing: 2003.

ONLINE SITES

The Susan B. Anthony House
http://www.susanbanthonyhouse.org

Not For Ourselves Alone: The Story of Susan B. Anthony and Elizabeth Cady Stanton
http://www.pbs.org/stantonanthony/sa_kids/-3k

The National Women's History Museum
http://www.nmwh.org

Index

Bold numbers indicate illustrations.

About the Author

Award-winning children's book author **Elaine Landau** has written more than two hundred nonfiction books for young readers. Ms. Landau has a bachelor's degree in English and journalism from New York University and a master's degree in Library and Information Science from Pratt Institute. Today, Ms. Landau lives in Miami, Florida, with her husband, Norman, and their son, Michael.